MW01656975

Comatose To Commander

A Driven Purpose in Overcoming the Odds Despite Being Black, Vulnerable, and Male in America

A Story to Inspire

by

KEVIN T. DAVIS, SR.

Lieutenant Commander

United States Navy, Retired

Printed in the United States of America
First Printing, 2017

ISBN: 978-1-5356-0779-7

Dedication

THIS BOOK IS DEDICATED TO all young people around the US (in general) but specifically is a call to all young black males. It is an intentional beckoning to encourage them to strive, fight and stretch to reach their fullest potential; to fulfill their destiny; to face and overcome the odds of what is (seemingly) a stack of bricks already piled high against them. By sharing the challenges I faced early in my life (on a quest **not** to become a statistic), I hope to speak volumes of how through sheer determination, drive, faith and belief in themselves, they (too) can overcome the odds. In revealing certain aspects of my life, I hope this book will inspire them to recognize the inner element of success that lies within and to stoke that element on the road toward achievement. Regardless of what everyone else has done or is doing, each young man needs to grasp ahold of that inner belief system that is tantamount to his success. The key is to never let your circumstances define who you are or what you can become in America. With sacrifice, hard work, resolve, and determination, a clear path of achievement will be created despite being **Black, Vulnerable and Male in America.**

Contents

Preface

Coma: a deep, prolonged unconsciousness, usually the result of disease, injury, or poison;

Comatose: marked by lethargy; torpid or torpor;

Lethargy: from the Greek word <lethargos>, forgetful; drowsy or sluggish indifference: apathy;

Torpid: having been deprived of the power of motion or feeling; dormant; hibernating;

Torpor: mental or physical inactivity;

Hibernating: to be in an inactive or dormant state or period.

Reflecting for a moment and allowing myself to digress, I now realize I was facing a defining moment in the face of adversity. As a young lad with his entire life ahead of him, I was dealt a blow that nearly derailed my future. What would I do? How would I rebound or would I succumb to a preconceived, inevitable fate? Perhaps the dagger would be the predestined one that awaited me in a seemingly hopeless situation? Society didn't seem to acknowledge that I was ***Black, Vulnerable and Male***, and perhaps, didn't bother to care. Somehow I managed to muster up an inner dignity to fight against the current on my way towards that island in the middle of an ocean, where I would define myself; be willing to work hard to evolve into that for which society thinks I may not have been predestined for, but for which I feel I was created. I knew there was a purpose in my being and I purposed to overcome the odds, despite being **Black, Vulnerable and Male in America.**

Let Me Tell You Something

Never did I imagine that one day I would be associated with the Executive Office of the President of the United States and ***a black man*** at that. Afterall, my life began with a twist that took me 46 years to figure out. Labeled and identified as having ADHD, with no medical knowledge to fully understand the societal implications of that designation, I decided to tell my story (both the "broken" side and the blessed side). I chose to take on this task with the hope that some young black male would draw inspiration from it and make a decision to succeed, despite being **Black, Vulnerable and Male in America.** It is my earnest desire that my brothers can look themselves in the mirror and realize they are more than gangbangers, hoods, and thugs. I want every young black youth to realize that although I didn't actually learn anything between ages seven and sixteen, I knew inside that I wasn't a total failure and a mess up. I felt this potential energy to fight back, to break through the brick wall that had been stacked against me from birth. Yes!

I wanted the millionaire status, the mansion, and the fast cars; to build a legacy my children would someday be proud of. I wanted more than just to be **Black, Vulnerable and Male in America.** I wanted to succeed... badly. So I am writing to encourage you today, young man (and young people in general), to make a decision, aim to reach through the sky and into the stratosphere, on your quest to evolve into the character or person of your dreams.

How It All Began

I WAS BORN A FRATERNAL twin, an unexpected, "surprise" child that my mother never had a clue she was carrying. She only knew she was pregnant with my brother but unknown to her, I was quietly developing within the recesses of my brother's bosom as if he was trying to hide me or keep me all to himself. Considering how big he was at birth, perhaps he was trying to have all of the nourishment for himself. Yet, on our birthdate and soon after he was delivered, I pressed my way forwards determined not to be left behind. My birth was totally unexpected especially since my brother had engulfed me in the womb. I was later told that my brother had wrapped himself around me as if I was a little pig in a blanket. Then, it was as if I suddenly unfurled, like a flower bud opening at the first hint of spring. There was no preconceived plan for me but nonetheless, here I was weighing in at a measly 3 pounds and to this day, my brother is bigger than me.

I do not recall being told how my mother received the news of just having given birth to twins but considering the way I was raised by Shirlena, it probably didn't faze her. Although she was already struggling with three others at home, she would muster up the strength to take care of Keith and me too. This would be the start of a life that would take me through a whirlwind of experiences but eventually away from the streets, drugs and violence of Baltimore city.

My entry into this world would be remarkable yet, as they say, it's not how you start but how you finish. The exact nature of my conception remains a mystery still to this day. I say mystery because aside from the eyes, my brother and I look absolutely nothing alike. I'm what they call high yellow with soft curly hair and Keith is brown-skinned, bald and favors Rev. Run (of Run DMC fame). While I cannot exactly explain the circumstances of our obvious differences or why I was unexpectantly born a twin, I do know that I was brought into this world to serve some meaningful purpose. It may have taken me some time to discover just what that is but truth be told and to a certain degree, I'm still evolving into it.

When I think about it, my introduction to this world is almost like the twin boys in the bible (Esau and Jacob). Jacob must have known he was special when he caught ahold of his brother's heel and wouldn't let go.

Like Jacob, I had an anointing on my life that nobody but the Lord knew. Only after unfortunate circumstances, trials and tribulations, is that anointing slowly and steadily being revealed. Since there were so many people who believed that nothing good came from the 'hoods and streets of inner city Baltimore, I became someone determined to be successful; determined to rise above my circumstances; determined to make a liar out of a system that claim a black man can't make it; determined to be a loving husband and father; determined to love somebody and myself; determined to overcome the odds. I adopted a belief that believing in yourself is your power and I purposed to use my belief to empower myself to another level of life.

The Early Years

I GREW UP IN A family of seven: four boys (Mark, Vernon, Keith and myself), two girls (Sernora and Mona) and of course, my mother, Shirlena. I recall neither having my father nor a father-figure in my life, although I'm told my mother once moved to Connecticut so I could be closer to "my dad". Unfortunately, I have no recollection of that time in my life. As a matter of fact, with the exception of my youngest sister, neither did any of my siblings. Although the man in the house (for a minute) was my youngest sister's dad, for my brothers and me that did not equate to much. There were no "father-son" baseball games; fishing trips; visits to the barbershop; or any other interaction you'd expect between a "father" and son. Nope. I can only remember my brothers, my sisters, me and my mom. There was no man in my life to protect me, teach me how to handle myself, teach me how to tie a tie, to clap at my sporting events or even to show how proud he was at my graduation. Coming of age and being aware of the opposite sex, there was no one to tell me about the "birds and the bees" or to show me what it was to be a "man". Nope. Everything I learned was at the behest of the streets and what they had to teach me. My mother was there, yeah, but she was working hard all the time to provide for us, making sure our meager needs were met. I appreciated her for that but I don't think she realized just how critical and valuable having a father or father-figure around is to a young boy. He is more than just how much money he makes and can buy you. He's more than just being a help with the bills or being able to fix things. No, having a father around embodies that character of "strength" that also shows he has enough love to want to be in your life; to watch you grow up and graduate from school; to feel proud as you mature into your own man. I didn't have one but I knew I wanted to be that father once I was finally on my own.

At the age of nine, I wish I had had that person, that father or father-figure in my life. I vividly recall how many issues and struggles my mom had to endure. Not only was there no one to help with the bills, but there was no man around to offer that protection and guidance to keep you and the family safe. I remember one day I was on my way to buy candy at the penny store. While crossing the street, ***thump***! I was hit hard by a car and left for dead right there in the middle of the street! I didn't see it coming… this terrible car accident that almost took my life. If a man had been with me, he might have been able to protect me by grabbing me or something, to keep me from being hit by that car. While I don't recall everything leading up to that horrific accident, I do remember my foot being stuck near the muffler as the car continued to drag me another 50 feet or so. When I finally became dislodged from that car, fractures all over my body, broken fingers, my face scraped up and covered in blood, going into survival mode was my only option. When the smoke finally cleared, fortunately God had sent an angel to rescue me. That stranger angel picked up my bloodied, fractured body, put me in his car and rushed me to the hospital. I actually never found out who this savior was because all I could remember was that he dropped me off at the hospital door and left! I may have never gotten to meet this person but I feel as though that guardian angel has always been with me, through both good and challenging situations. I obviously survived but it wasn't easy. I faced many challenges from that point on but in spite of it all, I knew (deep inside of me) that this wasn't going to be the end of my story.

Fractured Confidence

As a result of significant, traumatic head injuries (unknown to me) sustained in the accident, I remained in a coma for 3 months. Thank the Lord I recovered but not without some serious physical, emotional and mental challenges. I'm talking brain damage and chronic excruciating headaches, which continued into adulthood. These events preempted repeated failures, as my ability to conceptualize basic academics was a huge struggle for me. It played a significant role in reduced self-esteem and increased insecurities. Furthermore, I became susceptible to being ostracized and bullied. I really don't think my family fully understood my struggles coping with this accident yet I am sure they did the best they could to be compassionate and nurturing. In hindsight, it was almost as if they were misguided as to just how bad off I really was. Although it's clearer now why they felt the way they did (their apprehensions, concerns and worries in having to deal with my total recovery), as a young kid with issues you just want someone to hold and pacify you; to feel sorry for you and cater to your every whim and need. I understood it was hard enough trying to find the necessary means to support a child with serious physical and emotional needs but mental challenges too!? Now think about this for a moment…… when you're raised in a low income household with 5 other siblings, the ***last thing*** on anyone's mind is the mental health of a young black boy. I don't believe it was intentional but like I said, with my type of learning disabilities and impoverished surroundings, you learned to deal with problems by ignoring them as if they didn't exist. Hell, we were **already** striving to survive, trying to make ends meet. Later, my mother even told me to "hold down a job" just to help keep the lights on. They still got turned off but I purposed to stay positive, to press toward the next level on my way to success. Some of that "fractured confidence" still haunts me today but I purposed to rise above it. Although my beginnings were traumatized by events beyond my control, I always knew within the recesses of my mind that I was destined for success. Neither my unexpected arrival into this world nor the premonition of death (by way of the accident) were enough to obstruct my pathway to success. Sure there were obstacles, labels and discrimination; however, what the good Lord had for me, nothing or no one would stop.

Recovery and Discovery

After that terrible accident, it seemed my life would be derailed by an inability to learn. I began to struggle in school, with reading, writing, math and my speech. I found it very difficult to pronounce and understand the meaning of words. More than that, I was challenged in my use of words. My language was all screwed up and I couldn't talk right; well, at least not in the proper tense. It was all very challenging to me in a world that already deemed me a failure, even before I had gotten started. Furthermore, because of the perceived learning "disability", I was isolated away from my siblings and placed in "special" classes. Soon, I found myself becoming alienated and as a result, I became confrontational. In the guise of "defending" myself against a label, I found myself engaged in physical fights. Even my own family began to view me as a hard-headed, trouble making kid, for starting and becoming involved in so many fights. They couldn't figure me out and thought I used fighting to get attention but truth be told, I didn't want to be alone and away from my brothers and sisters. Being raised without a father around, I suppose I was hoping that someone would recognize this important element that was missing from my life. My behavior and antics stemmed from the fact I had no role model to walk before me and to hold me accountable. Consequently, my only avenue (I guess) was to draw from my surroundings that which was familiar to me. As much as I wanted to fend for believe in myself in the absence of a father, I later learned that while believing in yourself is a type of power, restraining yourself from negatively reacting in certain situations is your ***ultimate*** power.

Let me backtrack a moment to clarify something. The designation of "special" meant I had to endure riding the short, yellow school bus (alone) with a bunch of derelicts. I knew I didn't belong in that group! I wasn't that kind of "special". ***I got hit, doggone it!*** I was no longer comatose but I wanted people to know I was the way I was because of trauma and **not** because I wasn't smart or capable of learning. Believe me when I say I am not trying to justify my raucous and reckless behavior. I wanted and needed help but went about getting it the only way I knew how. My mom was too busy working and other things to provide for us that she may have simply not known how to get the help I needed; however, because of my erratic and aggressive behavior, the only solution (at that time) was to place me in special education classes. This ultimately associated me with the mentally challenged kids riding that short, yellow school bus! I know I had my issues but that was a huge mistake! Riding that bus made me an easy target for bullying. I mean, it subjected me to teasing; it took me through some emotional and embarrassing moments throughout both my childhood and early in my young adult life; it left me somewhat scarred. The insecurities of my learning disabilities coupled with the bullying and always being picked on, led me into a spiral of immature class clown behavior. And yes, I was involved in several fights a week. Suspended numerous times for those fights (along with being disrespectful to the teachers) didn't help my situation. First, I had a learning disability; now, I was this disruptive element in the classroom. Well, the easiest solution was to write me off and think slow-learning Kevin would never amount to anything. There was the perception that the (negative) environmental influences would somehow begin to take control of my life: hustling in the streets, becoming one of the neighborhood drug dealers, be dead or in jail by 18, or be a useless father with several kids running around the city. That type of stigma sticks with you and you start to believe that there's no hope, that that's your lot in life. Even my own siblings began to conjure thoughts of that being our destiny and feeling it was their duty to remind me (every day) of my expected outcome. It's hard to get out of that mode when you're living in a jungle but you know what? I can't blame them for not understanding my struggles (at the time). As I mentioned before, I never had any positive male role models in my younger years growing up and I doubt that they had too. They were only expressing to me what they knew, albeit limited to what (unfortunately) they had to learn on their own. My brothers and I didn't think about ethics, manhood or hard work, nor did we contemplate how it would all play a role later in our lives as adults. The lack of guidance even applied to my love life as I began to come of age (that's another chapter). The mere fact that I'm sharing this story is a testament to my decision to buck back against all of these odds and find my niche, anything, which would eventually propel me towards success. I was written off by all of my family members as hard-headed, stupid and useless, and that I would never amount to anything. Hell, if that's all you hear day in and day out, you start to believe that deceptive description.

Although I continued to deal with low self-esteem, low confidence and defensiveness right into young adulthood, I realized that I wanted more out of this life. I had always dreamed of being rich and owning a mansion, driving fancy cars and traveling the world. I began to embrace the idea that God had a bigger and better plan for me, just as I am sure He has for you, but here is the deal: you've got to press and not succumb to the notion that being ***Black, Vulnerable and Male in America*** is an inevitable death sentence! You are an overcomer! There is greatness inside of you! You are a force to be reckoned with! You are more than a blip in somebody's sentence. You are destined to overcome the odds if you just ***do not ever give up.*** You have to believe in hope. You cannot be ambitious without hope. Sure, having ambition does not always guarantee success but even a person living in poverty can feel great about waking up in the morning, having survived the terrors of the night. We don't always understand or know why people are in positions and situations they're in but we can all embrace the greatness in us and make a decision to change our destiny.

Sernora's Synopsis

My recollection of how life was for me would be considered one-sided if I didn't include the perspective of at least one of my siblings. My older sister, Sernora, faced her own set of difficulties but chose to take a chance on succeeding. She rose through the ranks of the Army Reserves in the arena of Information Technology and has managed communication sites in various capacities. She pulled herself up by the bootstraps, so to speak, and has done very well for herself. As a matter of fact, all of my siblings made the decision that life was not defined simply by our humble beginnings and impoverished surroundings. Baltimore city in general is a beautiful place, with much to offer; however, our world seemed bleak by comparison and we all simply wanted more.

Sernora was gracious enough to share her take on the obstacles and hurdles I faced from an early age, forming her own opinion of my desire and obsession with wanting to be successful:

When Kevin was born it was a surprise because Keith was wrapped around him. The pregnancy itself came as a bit of astonishment because there was no history of twins in the family. It was so much a startling turn of events that our great-grandmother caught four buses to come see them. They generated a lot of attention not only because they were the first set of twins but also because our mother was almost arrested behind them. They were so light at birth that when my mother was being discharged, the cops were called on her. What has her "crime"? Trying to kidnap two "white-looking babies"! Can you imagine?

My mother was a single parent, already raising three children in the projects of Baltimore and now there were a set of twins no one expected. Eventually, my mother cared for six children. Although times were difficult and very challenging, and sometimes there was hardly any food at the end of the month, we never went to bed hungry. Despite this fact, a lot of the family shied away from us when they learned of this. Consequently, we were hardly invited to any family gatherings but when we were, Shirlena always brought the meats! We, as "Shirlena's kids", were frowned upon and it was said that since nothing good came from the projects, nothing good was to become of us. She later graduated us away from the projects into a home and we all attained some level of success as adults. She always sensed something was wrong about how the family treated us but Shirlena couldn't articulate just what it was. Her primary focus was to make sure all of us were loved and subsequently, lived her life for her children.

In her own upbringing, Shirlena bore the brunt of caring for numerous brothers and sisters, being the oldest of thirteen. She had no childhood and really no adulthood. Her closest sister was Aunt Stephanie. I don't recall my mother sharing any of the pleasurable things she did or experienced in her younger days because as the oldest of her siblings, she had the responsibility of looking out for everybody else. She worked several odd jobs throughout her life but never stayed in any long enough to receive any type of "retirement" severance package, partly because of her responsibility to everyone but Shirlena. It was this fact that (I believe) made us all determined we were going to do things differently, especially Kevin. He always stood out as the one who would do things in a different light. He and mother seemed to be at odds over several issues, including how he would spend the money he earned. Her expectation was that he would bring the money to her (to help with the bills, food, etc.) but Kevin's ideal was "Why should I do that when it is your responsibility to take care of your kids?" Throughout it all, she denied herself simple pleasures that when the opportunity presented itself, she took the bait. Consequently, the very elements she sought to shield us from became the very elements that enchanted her. So at the level of the "empty nest", when she finally felt liberated, she later succumbed to those influences. Her feeling was that now it was time to "do Shirlena" since she had spent most of her life caring for everybody else. Unfortunately in deciding to "do" her, she paid the price prematurely with her life.

As oddly as Kevin's birth was, it seemed that he and Keith were either in competition with each other or determined to do just the opposite as twins. Keith was bigger than Kevin at birth, evidenced by Kevin's measly weight. Even today, Keith is larger in stature than Kevin. As for their personalities, they are opposites. Keith was more of the introvert while Kevin was Mr. Outgoing with an explosive personality. At the age of 5, Kevin had a certain temperament because he resented the "pretty boy and nice hair" assertions. Not that he was bad; he just had a very aggressive nature about himself. One time, that nature had gotten the best of him. When Kevin was age nine, we were all on our way to the corner store when he ran out into the street. A student driver saw him, panicked, took her hands off the wheel and struck him! He was hit so hard it knocked his shoes off. Screaming, a friend and I took him to the hospital. It didn't take long before everyone was asking what had happened to Kevin. Living in the projects had this one positive aspect: everyone knew everybody else. When that accident happened, there wasn't a single person who had not asked what had happened to Kevin. He remained comatose for about two and a half months but everybody was elated to see him when he returned home. Come to find out, the driver did not have insurance!

In spite of everything, there had always been some connection between Keith and Kevin. Keith and Kevin have always been close in spite of their competitive nature. Although they were separated for a short period of time during adolescence, the two of them were extremely close even though their personalities were strikingly different. Keith was the homebody and the favorite (mainly because he never questioned mom) but Kevin, on the other hand, was more the socialite hanging out with the wrong crowd. He had the "nice" hair and was this pretty, high yellow guy, but he always wanted people to know he was more than just a pretty face with nice hair. Opposed to the five of us, Kevin was more materialistic, stubborn, rebellious and brash, as if he had to prove himself. He was always going up against the grain and sometimes would be in conflict with our mom. If there was something he didn't agree with, Kevin would challenge her and end up in conflict with her. Of course, she considered this to be disrespectful and favored Keith because he was more docile.

Because of his intense drive to succeed, Kevin has always been very ambitious and we are all proud of how much of a success he has become, in light of our (and particularly his) very humble beginnings. Even as an enlisted Navy serviceman, people around him were always encouraging him to go back to school, to make education a priority. Despite the fact he graduated high school on a 5th grade reading level, the inner circle of the Navy's environment looked beyond that and saw something in him that influenced him to reach higher. Consequently, he went the officer route and we have never been more proud of him. Moreover, Kevin's older children (Kevin T., Jr and Valencia) are also very proud of their dad and only wished they were still together as a family (Kevin and his first wife divorced after 19 years of marriage. Sadly, Shirlena nor other family members never really embraced her because of her stand-offishness).

As I mentioned earlier, we never went to bed hungry because mom knew how to stir those pots! Regardless of the tensions that existed between Kevin and our mother, his accent in the culinary area of the Navy originated with Shirlena. When Kevin sat for the ASVAB exam, he only scored a 25! He barely made it in and was assigned to the galley, navy jargon for kitchen. As a matter of fact, with a score as low as his, he was actually supposed to be assigned to painting the ships; however, thankfully, some Captain took a liking to him. What seemed like a menial position when Kevin entered the Navy as a cook was actually the springboard catalyst to his eventual ascension into the position as the Director of White House Presidential Food Service. After all, it was our mom who prepped him. Now, he's building his brand and in a big way all because he never gave up on himself. In spite of living in impoverished conditions and dealing with challenging situations, Kevin never lost neither his verve nor his determination to find that key to success. He aroused from that coma with an inner drive and self-motivation unparalleled by anyone we know. Although our mom fell asleep shortly after his commissioning, she was instrumental in prepping him for a career and life that would reward him for his tenacity. She may not have had much in the way of goods but she did instill in him (and us) that he was somebody. He wanted more than what he had been exposed to and was willing to turn his life around from a troubled past.

Another important factor was the faith Kevin had. Although mother wasn't a church goer (she was deterred by a negative experience with a philandering pastor), she did establish a foundation for us which we carried into adulthood. It was that faith, coupled with hard work and sheer determination, which has contributed to Kevin's climb to success. Besides, he knew that one more year on the skid and he would have been either dead or in jail.

As for his military career as an officer, he was actually excited about the prospect of retiring at the highest level on the enlisted side. Although he later was excited about the possibility of becoming a naval officer, he was initially reluctant to accept the commission because of a complacent attitude. After all, considering how he started in life, attaining the ultimate enlisted appointment (as an E-9) into retirement would be all there was (for him). He later reconsidered the officer side of the branch when an inner circle of the navy environment began to encourage him to go back to school. Our mother was proud of how Kevin decided to turn the corner and find himself in the neighborhood of being an "Officer and a Gentleman". As I previously mentioned, unfortunately, she didn't live to witness his other successes. Reflecting on where he was and where he is now (and still "evolving"), as they say, "The rest is history".

The Choice To Succeed

In spite of how life started for me, even then I knew there was more to life than my circumstances predicated. Certainly, my pathway wasn't typical; however, a lot of successful people have traversed worse roads. The only difference between those who attain that level (they seek) and those who may fall short is faith, the inner drive and determination to overcome their odds. **There is a spiritual being within all of us that divine person inside of each of us that talks to us every day, we tend to either ignore it or do not acknowledge that it exists. Once we can acknowledge the spiritual being, we can truly embrace our hope, faith, strengths, courage, and once you have accepted this, you can open the door to limitless possibilities.** To every young male (particularly of the AA community), you too can choose to evolve into whatever and whoever you put your mind into becoming. ***Do not*** allow your circumstances to define you; ***do not*** let that which you cannot control master you; ***do not*** allow society to put shackles on your mind...the mind that the Creator designed specifically for you; ***do not*** allow a faulty educational system to place imposition and limits on what you expose your own mind to. Remember, I was hit and dragged by a car, comatose for three (3) months, placed in special education classes, bullied and ostracized. Yet, I made a decision to succeed. I chose to believe in myself. I chose to ***enlighten*** myself, to ***encourage*** myself, to ***empower*** myself, to ***evolve***. When it was all said and done, I found myself graduating from college with honors. Yes, honors! Remember, I graduated high school barely reading on a 5th grade level yet I chose to teach myself what I didn't "learn" in my younger years. Recall I said there was no learning for me between the ages of seven and sixteen. Although I was allowed to graduate reading only on a 5th grade level, it was in high school where the light came on, when I realized I had capabilities and made up my mind to focus. The same would be true of my ambition to pass the ASVAB in order to enter the US Navy. Everything is about a mindset and a strong determination to never give up hope, no matter how dismal and hopeless your current situation may seem. Nothing really significant has to happen. You just need to start pushing yourself toward that light called success. Besides, what have you got to lose!? Society is so ready to push you, young and black, off the edge you're already standing too close to. So chose to stand strong and push back not physically by bucking the system, but through your own mental resolve. Pick up a book, find your niche and dare yourself to succeed.

Doing the Best She Could

In spite of everything that happened during my earlier years, I really have to thank my mom for her tough love and her tenacious attitude towards me. That continued intrusion actually was a blessing to me. Growing up in a ruthless city known for its infamous murder rate among young black males and the lack of positive influential men in my life, I faced a conundrum of other negative attributes. Without my mom's never ending needling and meddling, I could have easily been victimized by a poor education system, the welfare government system, inadequate food and health care, malnutrition, hyperactivity, low attention deficiency, and bullying. Our gas and electric were always being disconnected; we were served with frequent eviction notices, and thus had no steady place to live. I was being raised in a single parent household with five other siblings in squalid conditions. I had no real outlet to get away from it all because I was considered too small for sports. Furthermore, among other elements, I was labeled ADHD and enrolled in special education classes, attaining only a 5th grade reading level while "graduating" high school. To top it off, I faced racial discrimination for being light-complexioned. Yet, in spite of all of this, my mother ensured I learned decent work ethics so I could hold my head high and continue to have my dignity whenever I was faced with adverse situations. She exposed all of us to hard work by refusing to let us stay in the house throughout the summer months and do nothing. No! She would lay the foundation that hard work and sacrifice were prerequisites to what you wanted in life. She wanted us to participate in keeping the lights on and food on the table. Sadly, the lights were still turned off and many times we didn't have enough to eat. We didn't go to bed without something but it seemed like I was never able to get full.

I actually started working at age 12, delivering papers and cutting grass, just to contribute something to the household. I would also carry groceries for little old ladies, who provided some extra change and sometimes, I would get a five-dollar bill! Later, at 14, my twin Keith and I found employment at a mental institution. That was an experience I would never forget. The people there were really disturbed and unkempt. Together, Keith and I must have changed over 100 beds and then fed the patients. In spite of the "messiness" and challenge of the situation, I learned valuable lessons in respecting everyone no matter their mental or physical state. As much as I wanted to quit working there, I had to look at the overall situation. My mother needed us to work to help pay for food and to keep the lights on! I must be honest and say, after working that hard to earn my own money, I was frustrated at the idea of giving my check to my mother. After all, as the adult, wasn't it ***her*** responsibility to pay the rent, keep on the lights and buy food!? I later viewed the situation differently and realized that my mom was doing the best that she could. Furthermore, there was another lesson I learned and that was, you have to do what it takes to help family!! If it takes everyone to get out there and get a job to help pay the bills, you do what you have to do and make sacrifices for the betterment of your family. These lessons in responsibility, hard work, perseverance and sacrifice continue to resonate with me today, and have been the very elements contributing to my successes in the White House.

The Decision

My CHOICE TO PURSUE A career in the United States Navy was a decision that would be the first of many that I'd make to take advantage of opportunities coming my way. Whatever presented itself as an avenue to catapult me to the next level in life, I would do my due diligence and pursue it; regardless of the fact that someone with my humble beginnings could have only dreamed of accomplishing the task. Yes, I know the Word says, "I can do all things…" but I never would have believed that applied to me given how I started. Sure, there have been many stories like mine but I endeavor to tell you of limitless possibilities as long as your focus remains on commitment. My journey has been long and hard but also a rewarding experience. I was and remain determined to overcome the odds, realizing early on that nothing comes easy but there's always a lesson to be learned in every struggle. Considering my early years of struggling to survive, read and simply pass school, life taught me to take notes. I mean, who would have ever thought a high-yellow, runt of a fellow out of inner city Baltimore, bullied and belittled, would survive the rigors of military life let alone become a commissioned officer?

Achieving the rank of Lieutenant Commander (LCDR) in the United States Navy was one of my many accomplishments. Earning my degree and graduating with honors was a farfetched idea to some who knew me way back when. To top it off, I was assigned to work as a Director of Food Services (in the Executive Office) as a member of the White House staff during President Obama's administration! If you had to judge by my traumatic beginnings, you would not have thought it possible. Neither did my mother, my siblings and certainly not me but that doesn't mean that they weren't in my corner pulling for me. In hindsight, I would not change a thing because I learned that the essence of perseverance, hard work, humility and sacrifice is the only recipe for success. When I joined the Navy back in 1988, I had ***no*** idea where my journey would take me. In my quest for success, I was simply looking for an adventure and an opportunity to move beyond my troubled environment and boy, oh boy, did I find one!

Even as I excelled in the Navy, there was another challenge I had to face. Perhaps it was inevitable on this stage as well, especially since I had already had a taste of it as a child. The big "D" word faced me yet again...

discrimination! The discrimination played a huge role in how I deal with other folks to this day. Yes, I experienced it in the Navy and still see manifestations of it. Heck, even the President has experienced it and unfortunately, it remained prevalent even during my tenure as a White House staffer. As a matter of fact, all throughout my career as a Naval Officer, discrimination had a way to raise its ugly head That's too bad because no matter the accomplishment, African-Americans will always face the inequity of having to work three times as hard as his white counterpart to compete on a seemingly level playing field. I had to fight for my reputation, despite presiding over multi-million dollar budgets; despite proving myself to showcase the presentation of food (masterfully) to dignitaries, both domestic and foreign; despite 28 years of experience and expertise in the Financial Logistics of Food Service Management; despite multiple awards as a expert food service manager; despite meeting deadlines on time-critical projects; despite presiding over multiple staff operatives both foreign and domestic. In light of all of these accomplishments (and more), it seems everytime you remain fixated on doing your best, achieving your goals, and building your brand, someone is always waiting in the wings to discredit you. Why? Because you're ***Black, Vulnerable and Male in America!*** No matter what (though), you must continue to prove "them" wrong every chance you get, in a tactful manner, because no one will listen to an undereducated, angry Black man. Discrimination is something a black man (and woman) will inevitably deal with at some point in their lives and careers. It doesn't disappear just because you are promoted or become the POTUS. No! Unfortunately, it's become a part of life itself. The best and most effective way to overcome this "disease" of discrimination (and racism) is to have your ducks in a row and be educated enough to recognize it. ***Step up*** when others step down; ***remain calm and in control*** when others become irate; ***be the bigger person*** and always, always think of yourself in a ***positive*** way. Every morning before I start my day, I read this anonymous note "Live the life you've always dreamed about, be fearless everything you do even in the face of adversity. Never stop learning use your imagination whenever possible. Recognize the **BE**auty that surrounds **YOU.** Always Remember where you came from, but never lose sight of where you are headed. Be the architect of your own destiny. Embrace the limitless possibilities of today and every day.

Young Love
Marriage & Divorce

WITHOUT ANY ADULT OR MATURE male role models in my life, it's no wonder I was never taught or learned how to interact with or respect a woman. Sadly, I witnessed several incorrect ways of how women (black women, in particular) were treated. The utter disrespect of women lead me onto a path of thinking of women as sexual objects, here to service my desires and needs, instead of as true queens and the very foundation of the black family. As I stated previously, there was no model for me to follow so I developed my own ideas of how to love a woman. I can only say that after I married my high school sweetheart, it was a lesson I didn't expect to end in divorce after 19 years of marriage.

I met my first wife at age 14, while working at the mental institution. I was so in love with her that I didn't know my left from my right. It's amazing how you can be so attracted to the opposite sex! That puppy love is some strong stuff!!! I would have (literally) jumped off a building for her and do anything to show my faithfulness to her. As a matter of fact, I wanted to get in good with her mother just to exemplify how I felt about her. If I bought her (my first wife) something, her mom would receive the same thing, whether it was flowers, candy, etc. (I have always respected her mom and although we have been divorced several years, I still hold her mother in high regard). In a sense, I always knew I loved her more than she loved me mainly because of how she treated me. I am not certain she actually knew how to love at all because of her troubled teenage years. Let's just say her "innocence" was taken far too young and she wore it on her face. She seemed a bit stand-offish but since I had my nose blown wide open, initially I didn't seem to care ***how*** she treated me. I was in love! I tried my best to "heal" her but I realized that a person has to want to be healed to move past the hurts. In spite of what we went through, we had two amazing kids together and I am proud to be the father of Valencia and Kevin Jr. I love my kids dearly and continue to work to build a brand into their future.

My wife and I had some really enjoyable moments together as young pups that fell in love early. As a result of that relationship, I developed a close, fatherly bond with my older children. Over the years since our divorce, looking at how I've relished, nurtured and grown into a mature relationship with our (now) young adults, I have no regrets. Although I wish things could have been different, my naval career was never really embraced by my ex-wife. For and to her, the culmination of life centered in, on and around Baltimore. She held no ambition to travel; and thus, had no desire to wholeheartedly love and support me. She lacked vision and remained of the mindset that you can never really grow away from familiar surroundings; hence, Baltimore was her mainstay both physically and mentally. Unfortunately, that very thought process contributed to the demise of our rela

Strong words of advice, Keep your focus on your ambitions and goals! If the woman truly cares for and loves you, she will understand and lend her support to you wholeheartedly. After all, she will reap the benefits of your sacrifice as well, and what better fulfillment than to spend the rest of your lives travelling, seeing the world and experiencing all that life has to offer both of you? My prayers to love again and have someone to support my hopes, dreams and re-build a foundation that experienced it's fair share of troubling times, were answered hence, I remarried the beautiful Dashana Davis and have fathered some amazing, outspoken ready to take on the world twins, Kristian and Kailyn. If there is a recipe for success when it comes to raising kids, some of the most important ingredients would have to include my wife's attributes of kindness, faith, courage, unconditional love, nurturer, and wittiness. They say behind every successful person, there's is a support system (family, pastor, and mentor) providing the support you need to grow into the person that already exist within you. They will always encourage you to follow your dreams.

Let Your Focus Be Your Guide

After the dissolution of my marriage, I began to refocus on my future. I knew that I would find love again but in preparation for that, I decided to look for an opportunity that would be the beginning of a legacy I'd leave behind for my children. As the title of this book indicates, I transcended from being in a coma to Commander. In the process of refocusing on my future, over time, I began to realize that my success was not tied simply to riches, fancy cars and worldwide travel. Instead, I embraced a new reality that happiness and achievement stemmed from how you play a part in the change you bring about in someone else's life (for the better). When I contemplated how to be that element of change for my family and helping others along the way, I decided to form the non-profit group ***Stratosphere Mentoring Services***. The organization mentors youngsters aged eight to adult, by ***Empowering*** and ***Encouraging*** them to ***Evolve,*** while they allow themselves to be ***Enlightened*** with the idea of developing into motivated, successful people. ***Stratosphere*** is committed to being instrumental in the areas of one-on-one mentoring through a Big

Brother, Big Sister Time concept; providing guidance and promoting confidential communication to discuss challenging situations they may be facing; creating positive change in youngsters lives by exposing them to limitless possibilities that exist within the cavities of their minds. Furthermore, a question is always posed: What have you done to serve your community? I want to be remembered as a person who cared, who made huge contributions to people around the world, despite not (at least not at the time of this writing) having attained millionaire status. My focal point of the organization expands to include

promoting health, wellness and fitness mentoring, especially as juvenile obesity remains a struggle amongst our youth; helping them become financially literate and to handle their money responsibly by learning to budget and invest; understanding that while school is a must, so is entertaining the idea of entrepreneurship and possibly owning their own businesses; and exercising the element of spiritual growth. As was said earlier, my mother may not have been much of a regular church attender (and neither am I), but she made sure I had a sense of purpose and a belief system, teaching me how to pray and be thankful for all blessings, no matter how small.

At the end of the day, how you live your life and if you lived it to fulfill your inner dreams and desires all boils down to if you did anything to be a blessing to another individual, another human.

Throughout my limited years on this earth, I've had some amazing mentors in my life that continue to teach me some valuable lessons in life.

Lesson One; Everyone can achieve excellence, all it takes is hard work, determination and sacrifices.

Lesson two; Reach for the stars if you don't' make it, at least you have someone you can admire that tried.

Lesson three; If you have a vision pursue it. Have no regrets.

Lesson Four; At the end of the day always think positive when it comes to racism, our similarities far outweigh our differences.

Lesson Five; It's not about how much money you make, it's about what you do with what you have already, now that's maximizing on the true riches of life!!!

Lesson Six; There are always two of you, there's the person you are now and there's the person you are driven to be. You will find yourself in competition with yourself, always pushing to achieve the excellence you were born to be.

Lesson Seven; Stop running to the finish line to win a race you already won. Look in your rearview mirror you can clearly see you are winning.

Lesson eight; You must enjoy the process of working on self, you are what you love, not what loves you.

Lesson nine; When you know how to think, it empowers you far beyond on what to think, be mindful of self.

Lesson ten; There is nothing wrong with getting dirty and working hard to achieve your goals.

Lesson eleven; Always seize to opportunity to succeed.

Lesson Twelve; Life is Non-refundable be better and always have a purpose.

Lesson; thirteen; It's easy to build strong children than repair broken adults.

Lesson fourteen; The world is a huge misunderstanding, don't waste a lot of time trying to understand it.

Lesson Fifteen; Don't be detrimental to your own growth.

Lesson sixteen; Opportunity comes to those who make it happen.

Lesson Seventeen; Nothing is left to chance, what happens is supposed to happened.

Lesson eighteen; When you have a fire from within, you are immune to the outsides forces that are trying to distract you and force you to change directions.

Lesson nineteen; As you continue your path to enlightenment it will bring clarity in your life, seeking knowledge of self is the key to happiness.

Lesson twenty; Yesterday is beautiful reflection, today is a new beginning and tomorrow is a limitless possibility.

Pathway To Enlightenment

My path to enlightenment started long before I joined the Navy in 1988. It was a journey that would take me to the war torn country of Afghanistan, one that was lonely and depressing, with feelings of hopelessness. There I was in this remote foreign environment, not knowing what my destiny would be. Yet, I was determined that somehow, I would salvage what remained of my sanity and get through it.

Flashing back to when I was separated from my brothers (and made to ride that short yellow school bus), in a sense, I felt a sort of reigniting or urge for attention begin to well up in me again. It was a different environment and surroundings, yet a similar feeling. Signing up for the military, I realized that a time such as this was imminent, however, being lonely in the middle of a desert, involved in a "war" that was none of our business, was pretty darn depressing...even if it wasn't Baltimore. Having made up my mind that I would make it, I experienced an awakening of sort. Never did I imagine that

I would encounter a group of men who were seemingly God sent. I mean, here I was missing my brothers and these young men would help me build a foundation of peace, harmony and forgiveness, of both myself and my country. The world I found myself living in at that time was not the world I wanted to be in; however, it must have been kismet that my eyes would be opened to see the light. At that moment in my life, I began to embrace a change of my mind to identify with the positive thoughts held within. Thus, I purposely retrained my mind by clearing it of negative thoughts, channeling my focus on my path to enlightenment.

The journey is not for the fainthearted as it requires self-examination, humility, commitment and fellowship. My "calling" to receive this gracious gift required me to study, memorize and apply my learning to a board of great examiners. By choosing to become a Master Mason, my hope was restored in both mankind and brotherhood. Understand that the state of mind I was in when the invitation was extended to me was one of destitution. Yet, to be in the presence of so many God-fearing men willing to submit to a higher power than themselves, demonstrated something to me that I wanted to be a part of. I learned that the humility associated with the Masonic journey is really all about preparation of one's heart. Make no mistake about it. Becoming a raised

Master Mason was not the end in and of itself, far from it. Instead, this was merely an initiation to what would be my true destiny....becoming an asset to my fellow man. The symbolic presence of our world continually reminds a Master Mason that his temple must always be opened to and governed by Wisdom, Respect, Growth and Sacrifice. No explanation is required for those who understand. For those who cannot comprehend this, no explanation is possible. Yet and still, for those wanting to understand, experiencing the explanation would help you along your path to enlightenment.

As previously stated, one must understand the state of my mind when the invitation to participate in the experience was extended to me by my brothers. They lifted me up from a dark place and encouraged me to walk towards the light. I now realize my destiny was always hidden in plain view and have become empowered since accepting that journey. As my light shines brighter and brighter each day, my hope continues. As I continually seek knowledge, I find myself growing as a person, my light illuminating with greater abundance. If this journey is for you, always seek knowledge and truth, and never be afraid to grow spiritually on a quest towards greatness.

The Culmination

ALTHOUGH MY BEGINNINGS WERE TRAUMATIZED by events beyond my control, I always knew within the recesses of my mind that I was destined for success. Neither my unexpected arrival into this world nor the premonition of death were enough to obstruct me from my destiny. Sure there were obstacles, labels and discrimination; however, what good the Lord had for me, nothing or no one would stop the flow. My life sustained the derailment of my ability to learn but it would serve to catapult me into the stratosphere of possibilities. Never did anyone imagine that slow-learning Kevin would amount to anything, let alone a commanding officer, within the spectrum of the highest office in the land. My pathway wasn't typical; but then again, a lot of successful people have traversed far worse roads. The only difference between those who attain that level of success (they seek) and those who fall short is the inner determination to overcome the odds.

To every young person reading this book (and particularly, African American males), you too can choose to evolve into whatever you put your mind into becoming. Do not let your circumstances define you. Do not let that which you cannot control, master and have control over you. Do not allow society to put shackles on your mind, the mind that the Creator designed specifically for you. Do not allow a faulty educational system to limit what you expose your own mind to. Remember, I was hit and dragged by a car, comatose for three (3) months, placed in special education classes, bullied and ostracized. YET! I made a decision to succeed! I chose to believe in myself. I chose to enlighten myself, to evolve. After all is said and done, my graduating from college with honors, is the greatest testament to what can be achieved, if you choose to.....despite being **Black, Vulnerable and Male in America.**

No Words Necessary

Devotion
LOVE
TRUST
ALWAYS
be happy
UNITY
thankful
HOME
memories
HONESTY
forever
Family
unique
bless
FAITH
CHERISHED
LISTEN
RESPECT
TOGETHER
HOPE
STRENGTH
MARRIAGE
Treasure
HEART
Warmth
traditions
Laughter
relationship
HUG
KIND
Smile
HONOR
adore
Kiss
Romance

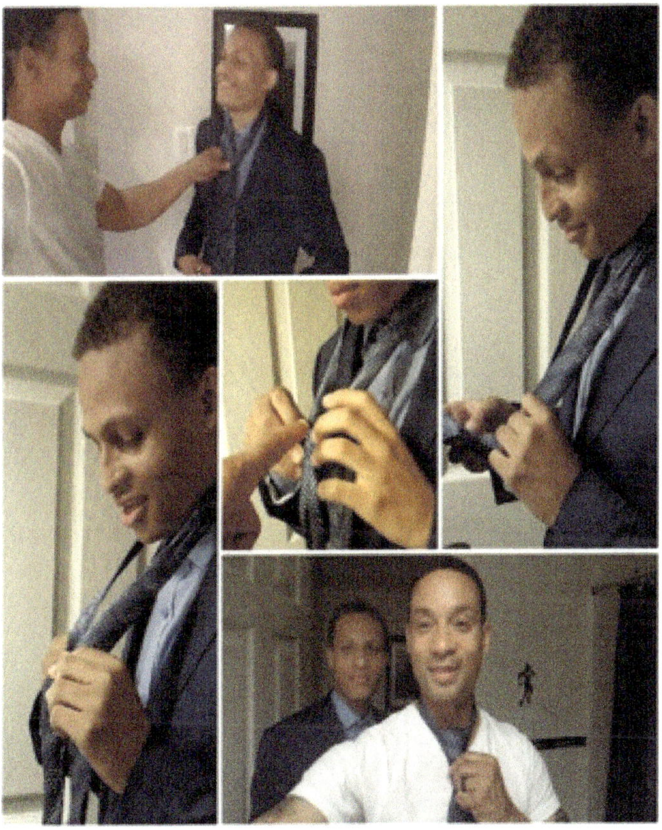

THE WHITE HOUSE

WASHINGTON

April 8, 2013

Dear LT Davis,

Congratulations on your selection as the next Director, Presidential Food Service. During the interviews at the White House, without exception, each person you interviewed with commented on your professional and confident manner of presentation.

Your nomination to be the Director, Presidential Food Service reflects the high regard in which you are held. I know your experience at the White House will be both enjoyable and rewarding.

We in the Military Office look forward to your arrival and if there is anything we can do to assist you, please do not hesitate to contact us at (202) 757-2151.

Sincerely,

GEORGE D. MULLIGAN
Deputy Assistant to the President and
Director, White House Military Office

LT Kevin T. Davis, USN
2014 Docklanding Court
Suffolk, VA 23435

SEAL OF THE PRESIDENT OF THE UNITED

THE UNITED STATES
UNITED STATES OF AMERICA

SEAL OF THE PRESIDENT OF THE UNITED STATES

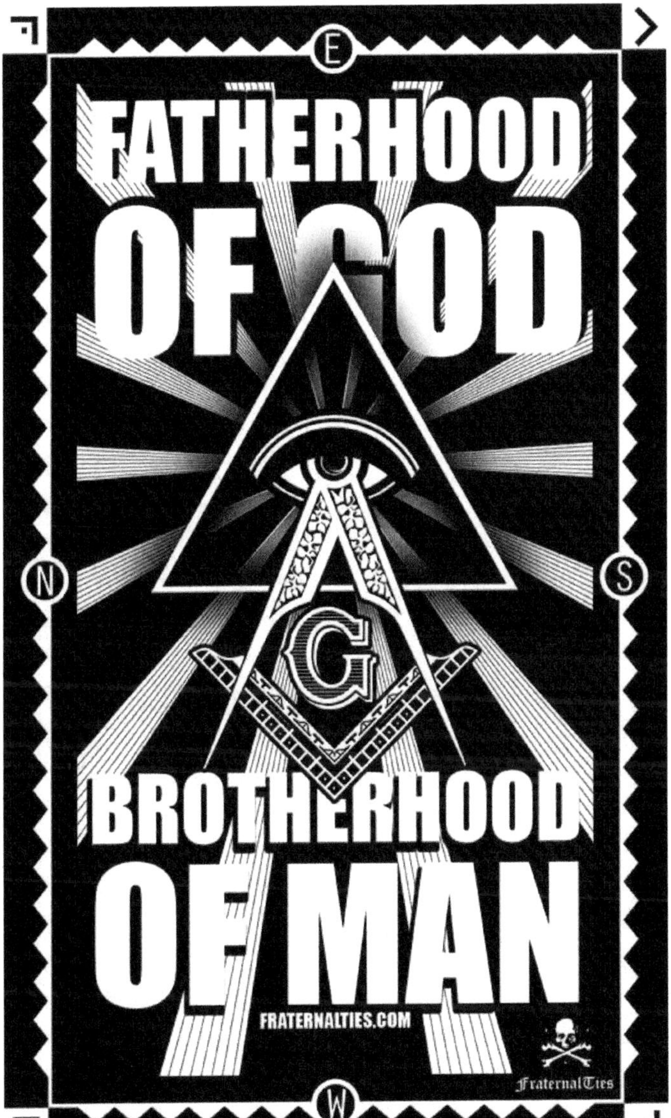
E
FATHERHOOD
OF GOD
N
S
G
BROTHERHOOD
OF MAN
FRATERNALTIES.COM
FraternalTies
W

G
02/ 19/ 2007

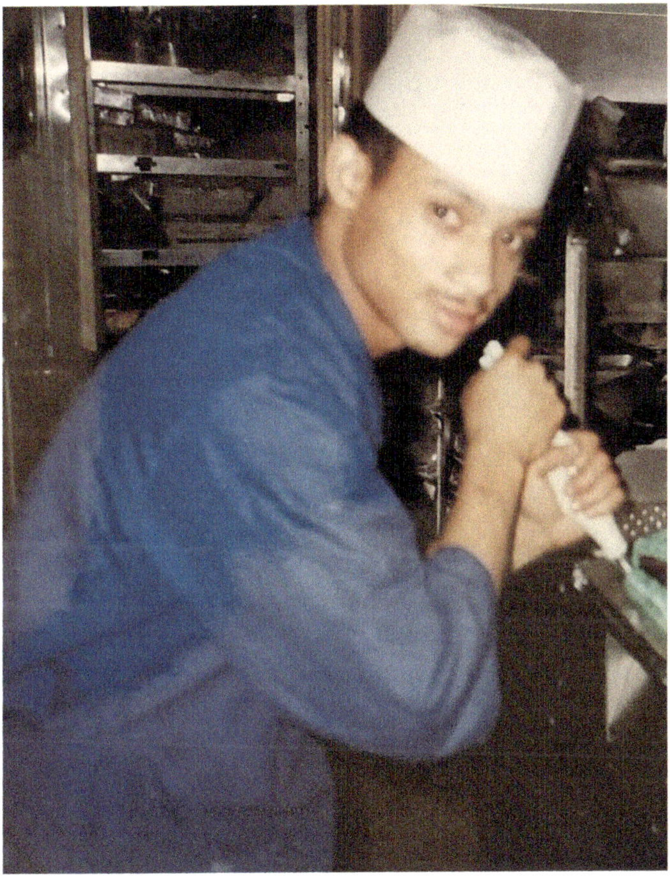

I guess you can say I woke up.

"Comatose to Commander"

Four Pillars of Success

EMPOWER-ENCOURAGE-ENLIGHTEN-EVOLVE

THESE FOUR WORDS BECAME THE staple of ***STRATOSPHERE Mentoring Services, INC***, a non-profit group I organized and founded in 2016. They embody a spirit of accomplishment, despite being **Black, Vulnerable and Male in America.** I had ***A Driven Purpose*** to succeed, a quest to ***Overcome the Odds***, despite being a black man living in America. Who would have ever thought that a 9 yr. old black boy from Baltimore, Maryland, known for its' blight of boarded up buildings, poverty and seemingly never ending street violence, who was violently struck and dragged by a car, left for dead, faced with learning challenges, a victim of bullying, growing up without a father and mislabeled as a gangbanger, would ever overcome impressionable odds to become a high ranking naval officer, personally and proudly serving the first African-American POTUS? Furthermore, whoever would have thought that a naval career would not only be the beginning of a transition but be a means by which I would begin to build my own brand? It has been widely acclaimed that it's not how you start but how you finish and although I am far from finished (actually, I am just beginning), a career that started in the galley has catapulted me into branding KEVCO Enterprises, a 5-Star Food Service Management and Logistics Consulting Company. The opportunity to literally and figuratively serve my country permitted me to be in a position to network and brainstorm with a slew of very accomplished people, from politicians to corporate business owners, sports All-Stars and Hall-of-Famers. Who would have ever thought? Yet, from the brokenness of Baltimore City, here I am Kevin T. Davis Sr, having done just that and aspiring to do even more.

CPSIA information can be obtained
at www.ICGtesting.com
Printed in the USA
BVOW11s0141200118
505484BV00010BA/53/P

9 781535 607797